THE STORY
of JESUS
for Kids

SELECTIONS FROM THE
NEW INTERNATIONAL
READER'S VERSION

Library of Congress Catalog Card Number 2010943071

Contents

1

The Birth of the King

John wrote about Jesus by calling him "the Word." Whenever you hear or read "the Word," you can replace it with "Jesus." Here's what John wrote:

In the beginning, the Word was already there. The Word was with God, and the Word was God. He was with God in the beginning. All things were made through him. Nothing that has been made was made without him. Life was in him, and that life was the light for all people.

The light shines in the darkness. But the darkness has not overcome the light.

The true light that gives light to everyone was coming into the world. The Word was in the world. And the world was made through him. But the world did not recognize him. He came to what was his own. But his own people did not accept him. Some people did accept him and did believe in his name. He gave them the right to become children of God. To be a child of God has nothing to do with human parents. Children of God are not born because of human choice or because a husband wants them to be born. They are born because of what God does.

The Word became a human being. He made his home with us. We have seen his glory. It is the glory of the One and Only, who came from the Father. And the Word was full of grace and truth.

In the past, God gave us grace through the law of Moses. Now, grace and truth come to us through Jesus Christ. No one has ever seen God. But the One and Only is God and is at the Father's side. The one at the Father's side has shown us what God is like.

The Birth of the King

Here is the story of Jesus' birth according to Luke:

God sent the angel Gabriel to Nazareth, a town in Galilee. He was sent to a virgin. The girl was engaged to a man named Joseph. He came from the family line of David. The virgin's name was Mary. The angel greeted her and said, "The Lord has blessed you in a special way. He is with you."

Mary was very upset because of his words. She wondered what kind of greeting this could be. But the angel said to her, "Do not be afraid, Mary. God is very pleased with you. You will become pregnant and give birth to a son. You must call him Jesus. He will be great and will be called the Son of the Most High God. The Lord God will make him a king like his father David of long ago. The Son of the Most High God will rule forever over his people. They are from the family line of Jacob. That kingdom will never end."

"How can this happen?" Mary asked the angel. "I am a virgin."

The angel answered, "The Holy Spirit will come to you. The power of the Most High God will cover you. So the holy one that is born will be called the Son of God."

"I serve the Lord," Mary answered. "May it happen to me just as you said it would." Then the angel left her.

Mary said,

"My soul gives glory to the Lord.
　My spirit delights in God my Savior.
He has taken note of me
　even though I am not considered
　　important.
From now on all people will call me
　　blessed.
　The Mighty One has done great things
　　for me.
　His name is holy.
He shows his mercy to those who have
　　respect for him,
　from parent to child down through the
　　years.
He has done mighty things with his
　　powerful arm.
　He has scattered those who are proud
　　in their deepest thoughts.

He has brought down rulers from their
thrones.
But he has lifted up people who are not
considered important.
He has filled with good things those who
are hungry.
But he has sent away empty those who
are rich.
He has helped the people of Israel, who
serve him.
He has always remembered to be kind
to Abraham and his children down through
the years.
He has done it just as he promised to
our people of long ago."

*Although Joseph and Mary were
engaged, they weren't married yet, and
neither one had ever tried to have a baby.
So when Mary told Joseph she was pregnant, Joseph was surprised. After all, Mary
was the first and only woman God made
pregnant this special way.*

Her husband Joseph was faithful to the law.
But he did not want to put her to shame in public. So he planned to divorce her quietly.

But as Joseph was thinking about this, an angel of the Lord appeared to him in a dream. The angel said, "Joseph, son of David, don't be afraid to take Mary home as your wife. The baby inside her is from the Holy Spirit. She is going to have a son. You must give him the name Jesus. That's because he will save his people from their sins."

All this took place to bring about what the Lord had said would happen. He had said through the prophet, "The virgin is going to have a baby. She will give birth to a son. And he will be called Immanuel." *(Isaiah 7:14)* The name Immanuel means "God with us."

Joseph woke up. He did what the angel of the Lord commanded him to do. He took Mary home as his wife.

In those days, Caesar Augustus made a law. It required that a list be made of everyone in the whole Roman world.

Everyone went to their own town to be listed.

So Joseph went also. He went from the town of Nazareth in Galilee to Judea. That is where

Bethlehem, the town of David, was. Joseph went there because he belonged to the family line of David. He went there with Mary to be listed. Mary was engaged to him. She was expecting a baby. While Joseph and Mary were there, the time came for the child to be born. She gave birth to her first baby. It was a boy. She wrapped him in large strips of cloth. Then

she placed him in a manger. That's because there was no guest room where they could stay.

There were shepherds living out in the fields nearby. It was night, and they were taking care of their sheep. An angel of the Lord appeared to them. And the glory of the Lord shone around them. They were terrified. But the angel said to them, "Do not be afraid. I bring you good news. It will bring great joy for all the people. Today in the town of David a Savior has been born to you. He is the Messiah, the Lord. Here is how you will know I am telling you the truth. You will find a baby wrapped in strips of cloth and lying in a manger."

Suddenly a large group of angels from heaven also appeared. They were praising God. They said,

"May glory be given to God in the highest heaven!
And may peace be given to those he is pleased with on earth!"

The angels left and went into heaven. Then the shepherds said to one another, "Let's go to Bethlehem. Let's see this thing that has happened, which the Lord has told us about."

So they hurried off and found Mary and Joseph and the baby. The baby was lying in the manger. After the shepherds had seen him, they told everyone. They reported what the angel had said about this child. All who heard it were amazed at what the shepherds said to them. But Mary kept all these things like a secret treasure in her heart. She thought about them over and over. The shepherds returned. They gave glory and praise to God. Everything they had seen and heard was just as they had been told.

After Jesus' birth, Wise Men from the east came to Jerusalem. They asked, "Where is the child who has been born to be king of the Jews? We saw his star when it rose. Now we have come to worship him."

When King Herod heard about it, he was very upset. Everyone in Jerusalem was troubled too.

King Herod was afraid Jesus would become king instead of him. So he decided to get rid of Jesus. When God told Joseph what Herod wanted to do, he moved his

family to Egypt so Jesus would be safe.
When Herod finally died, they moved back
home.

Every year Jesus' parents went to Jerusalem for the Passover Feast. When Jesus was 12 years old, they went up to the feast as usual. After the feast was over, his parents left to go back home. The boy Jesus stayed behind in Jerusalem. But they were not aware of it. They thought he was somewhere in their group. So they traveled on for a day. Then they began to look for him among their relatives and friends. They did not find him. So they went back to Jerusalem to look for him. After three days they found him in the temple courtyard. He was sitting with the teachers. He was listening to them and asking them questions. Everyone who heard him was amazed at how much he understood. They also were amazed at his answers. When his parents saw him, they were amazed. His mother said to him, "Son, why have you treated us like this? Your father and I have been worried about you. We have been looking for you everywhere."

"Why were you looking for me?" he asked.

"Didn't you know I had to be in my Father's house?" But they did not understand what he meant by that.

Then he went back to Nazareth with them, and he obeyed them. But his mother kept all these things like a secret treasure in her heart. Jesus became wiser and stronger. He also became more and more pleasing to God and to people.

Discussion Questions

1. Is there someone in your life who has a baby or young child? Do you know what you were like as a baby or young child? Tell a story about yourself that you have heard someone else tell about you, or talk about a memory you have of yourself as a young child.

2. Have you ever gotten lost? How did it happen and what did you do?

3. How can you become "more pleasing to God and to people" (like Jesus as he grew up)?

2
Jesus' Ministry Begins

The Bible doesn't tell us what Jesus did between the ages of 12 and 30. Jesus probably learned to be a carpenter like Joseph, and he probably played with his friends. One of his friends might have been his cousin John. John was a very special person to God too. Around the time Mary was visited by the angel, the same angel came to tell John's parents that John would be

born soon. And the angel also said John would tell the world the Messiah—Jesus— had finally come.

In those days John the Baptist came and preached in the Desert of Judea. He said, "Turn away from your sins! The kingdom of heaven has come near."

John's clothes were made out of camel's hair. He had a leather belt around his waist. His food was locusts and wild honey. People went out to him from Jerusalem and all Judea. They also came from the whole area around

the Jordan River. When they confessed their sins, John baptized them in the Jordan.

Jesus came from Galilee to the Jordan River. He wanted to be baptized by John. But John tried to stop him. So he told Jesus, "I need to be baptized by you. So why do you come to me?"

Jesus replied, "Let it be this way for now. It is right for us to do this. It carries out God's holy plan." Then John agreed.

As soon as Jesus was baptized, he came up out of the water. At that moment heaven was opened. Jesus saw the Spirit of God coming down on him like a dove. A voice from heaven said, "This is my Son, and I love him. I am very pleased with him."

The Holy Spirit led Jesus into the desert. There the devil tempted him. After 40 days and 40 nights of going without eating, Jesus was hungry. The tempter came to him. He said, "If you are the Son of God, tell these stones to become bread."

Jesus answered, "It is written, 'Man must not live only on bread. He must also live on every word that comes from the mouth of God.'"

(Deuteronomy 8:3)

Then the devil took Jesus to the holy city. He had him stand on the highest point of the temple. "If you are the Son of God," he said, "throw yourself down. It is written,

> " 'The Lord will command his angels to take
> good care of you.
> They will lift you up in their hands.
> Then you won't trip over a stone.' "
>
> *(Psalm 91:11,12)*

Jesus answered him, "It is also written, 'Do not test the Lord your God.' " *(Deuteronomy 6:16)*

Finally, the devil took Jesus to a very high mountain. He showed him all the kingdoms of the world and their glory. "If you bow down and worship me," he said, "I will give you all this."

Jesus said to him, "Get away from me, Satan! It is written, 'Worship the Lord your God. He is the only one you should serve.' " *(Deuteronomy 6:13)*

Then the devil left Jesus. Angels came and took care of him.

After Jesus was tempted in the desert, he started to preach to the people. Meanwhile, John the Baptist kept telling the people to listen to Jesus because he was the Messiah. But some of the Jewish leaders didn't believe John was telling the truth.

The Jewish leaders in Jerusalem sent priests and Levites to ask John who he was. John spoke the truth to them. He did not try to hide the truth. He spoke to them openly. He said, "I am not the Messiah."

They asked him, "Then who are you? Are you Elijah?"

He said, "I am not."

"Are you the Prophet we've been expecting?" they asked.

"No," he answered.

They asked one last time, "Who are you? Give us an answer to take back to those who sent us. What do you say about yourself?"

John replied, using the words of Isaiah the prophet. John said, "I'm the messenger who is calling out in the desert, 'Make the way for the Lord straight.'" *(Isaiah 40:3)*

The Pharisees who had been sent asked him, "If you are not the Messiah, why are you baptizing people? Why are you doing that if you aren't Elijah or the Prophet we've been expecting?"

"I baptize people with water," John replied. "But someone is standing among you whom you do not know. He is the one who comes after me. I am not good enough to untie his sandals."

This all happened at Bethany on the other side of the Jordan River. That was where John was baptizing.

The next day John saw Jesus coming toward him. John said, "Look! The Lamb of God! He takes away the sin of the world! This is the one I was talking about. I said, 'A man who comes after me is more important than I am. That's because he existed before I was born.' I did not know him. But God wants to make it clear to Israel who this person is. That's the reason I came baptizing with water."

Then John told them, "I saw the Holy Spirit come down from heaven like a dove. The Spirit remained on Jesus. I myself did not know him. But the one who sent me to baptize with water told me, 'You will see the Spirit come down and remain on someone. He is the one who will baptize with the Holy Spirit.' I have seen it happen. I am a witness that this is God's Chosen One."

Jesus was ready to start his ministry now and tell the people that he was the Messiah who would save them from all their sins if they would confess and believe. Jesus wanted helpers who would learn from him. These helpers, called disciples, went with Jesus practically everywhere. They saw Jesus do some very amazing things. Simon, one of Jesus' disciples, was worried about his mother-in-law. He told Jesus that she was ill.

So [Jesus] went to her. He took her hand and helped her up. The fever left her. Then she began to serve them.

That evening after sunset, the people brought to Jesus all who were sick. They also brought all who were controlled by demons. All the people in town gathered at the door. Jesus healed many of them. They had all kinds of sicknesses. He also drove out many demons. But he would not let the demons speak, because they knew who he was.

A man who had a skin disease came to Jesus. On his knees he begged Jesus. He said,

"If you are willing to make me 'clean,' you can do it."

Jesus became angry. He reached out his hand and touched the man. "I am willing to do it," Jesus said. "Be 'clean'!" Right away the disease left the man, and he was "clean."

Jesus sent him away at once. He gave the man a strong warning. "Don't tell this to anyone," he said. "Go and show yourself to the priest. Offer the sacrifices that Moses commanded. It will be a witness to the priest and the people that you are 'clean.'" But the man went out and started talking right away. He spread the news to everyone. So Jesus could no longer enter a town openly. He stayed outside in lonely places. But people still came to him from everywhere.

A few days later, Jesus entered Capernaum again. The people heard that he had come home. So many people gathered that there was no room left. There was not even room outside the door. And Jesus preached the word to them. Four of those who came were carrying a man who could not walk. But they could not get him close to Jesus because of the crowd.

So they made a hole by digging through the roof above Jesus. Then they lowered the man through it on a mat. Jesus saw their faith. So he said to the man, "Son, your sins are forgiven."

Some teachers of the law were sitting there. They were thinking, "Why is this fellow talking like that? He's saying a very evil thing! Only God can forgive sins!"

Right away Jesus knew what they were thinking. So he said to them, "Why are you thinking these things? Is it easier to say to this man, 'Your sins are forgiven'? Or to say, 'Get up, take your mat and walk'? But I want you to know that the Son of Man has authority on earth to forgive sins." So Jesus spoke to the man who could not walk. "I tell you," he said, "get up. Take your mat and go home." The man got up and took his mat. Then he walked away while everyone watched. All the people were amazed. They praised God and said, "We have never seen anything like this!"

The Pharisees were angry with Jesus because they didn't think he was telling the truth. Jesus was saying he could for-give people's sins, which was something only God could do. The Pharisees didn't think there was any way that Jesus could be the Messiah.

Jesus traveled all over Israel preaching and doing miracles. Before long, huge crowds gathered around him wherever he went.

News about him spread all over Syria. People brought to him all who were ill with different kinds of sicknesses. Some were suffering great pain. Others were controlled by demons. Some were shaking wildly. Others couldn't move at all. And Jesus healed all of them. Large crowds followed him. People came from Galilee, from the area known as the Ten Cities, and from Jerusalem and Judea. Others came from the area across the Jordan River.

Because of the crowd, Jesus told his disciples to get a small boat ready for him. This would keep the people from crowding him. Jesus had healed many people. So those who were sick were pushing forward to touch him. When people controlled by evil spirits saw him, they fell down in front of him. The spirits shouted, "You are the Son of God!" But Jesus ordered them not to tell people about him.

Jesus didn't want to tell everyone he was the Messiah too quickly, because he first had to teach them what the Messiah had come to do: save the people from sin, not destroy Rome in a battle. Jesus knew that he had to do a lot of teaching to make the people see who the Messiah really was. But first he had to teach his helpers.

Jesus went up on a mountainside. He called for certain people to come to him, and they came. He appointed 12 of them so that they would be with him. He would also send them out to preach. And he gave them authority to drive out demons.

After this, Jesus traveled around from one town and village to another. He announced the good news of God's kingdom. His 12 disciples were with him. So were some women who had been healed of evil spirits and sicknesses. One was Mary Magdalene. Seven demons had come out of her. Another was Joanna, the wife of Chuza. He was the manager of Herod's household. Susanna and many others were there also. These women were helping to support Jesus and the 12 disciples with their own money.

Discussion Questions

1. How can you tell people about Jesus? (Brainstorm some options like blogging, writing in a journal, or working with the children's groups at church.)

2. Do you think you would enjoy eating locusts and honey like John the Baptist? Do you think John enjoyed it? What are your least favorite foods? What about your favorites?

3. Have you ever been tempted to do something you know God would not like? What did you do about the temptation?

4. After reading this chapter, what do you think of Jesus?

3

No Ordinary Man

The Pharisees were important teachers. They followed all of the rules God had told the Israelites to follow when they were in the desert. The Pharisees even added more rules to follow, and they wanted the people to live the exact same way. But now that the Messiah had come, Jesus' task was to teach some new ideas to the people.

Jesus often used stories—called parables—to teach the people. Parables are *stories with a special meaning about the kingdom of heaven. God wanted Jesus to teach the people how to live out the kingdom of heaven on earth.*

Jesus said, "What can we say God's kingdom is like? What story can we use to explain it? It is like a mustard seed, which is the smallest of all seeds on earth. But when you plant the seed, it grows. It becomes the largest of all garden plants. Its branches are so big that birds can rest in its shade."

Using many stories like these, Jesus spoke the word to them. He told them as much as they could understand. He did not say anything to them without using a story. But when he was alone with his disciples, he explained everything.

The tax collectors and sinners were all gathering around to hear Jesus. But the Pharisees and the teachers of the law were whispering among themselves. They said, "This man welcomes sinners and eats with them."

Then Jesus told them a story. He said, "Suppose one of you has 100 sheep and loses one of them. Won't he leave the 99 in the open country? Won't he go and look for the one lost sheep until he finds it? When he finds it, he will joyfully put it on his shoulders and go home. Then he will call his friends and neighbors together. He will say, 'Be joyful with me. I have found my lost sheep.' I tell you, it will be the same in heaven. There will be great joy when one sinner turns away from sin. Yes, there will be more joy than for 99 godly people who do not need to turn away from their sins."

One day an authority on the law stood up to test Jesus. "Teacher," he asked, "what must I do to receive eternal life?"

"What is written in the Law?" Jesus replied. "How do you understand it?"

He answered, "'Love the Lord your God with all your heart and with all your soul. Love him with all your strength and with all your mind.' *(Deuteronomy 6:5)* And, 'Love your neighbor as you love yourself.'" *(Leviticus 19:18)*

"You have answered correctly," Jesus replied. "Do that, and you will live."

But the man wanted to make himself look

good. So he asked Jesus, "And who is my neighbor?"

Jesus replied, "A man was going down from Jerusalem to Jericho. Robbers attacked him. They stripped off his clothes and beat him. Then they went away, leaving him almost dead. A priest happened to be going down that same road. When he saw the man, he passed by on the other side. A Levite also came by. When he saw the man, he passed by on the other side too. But a Samaritan came to the place where the man was. When he saw the man, he felt sorry for him. He went to him, poured olive oil and wine on his wounds and bandaged them. Then he put the man on his own donkey. He brought him to an inn and took care of him. The next day he took out two silver coins. He gave them to the owner of the inn. 'Take care of him,' he said. 'When I return, I will pay you back for any extra expense you may have.'

"Which of the three do you think was a neighbor to the man who was attacked by robbers?"

The authority on the law replied, "The one who felt sorry for him."

Jesus told him, "Go and do as he did."

Jesus didn't always tell stories; instead he sometimes preached sermons to the people. He gave this next sermon when a crowd was gathered on a mountainside.

He said,

"Blessed are those who are spiritually
          needy.
    The kingdom of heaven belongs to them.
Blessed are those who are sad.
    They will be comforted.
Blessed are those who are humble.
    They will be given the earth.
Blessed are those who are hungry and
          thirsty for what is right.
    They will be filled.
Blessed are those who show mercy.
    They will be shown mercy.
Blessed are those whose hearts are pure.
    They will see God.
Blessed are those who make peace.
    They will be called children of God.
Blessed are those who suffer for doing
          what is right.
        The kingdom of heaven belongs to
          them.

"Blessed are you when people make fun of you and hurt you because of me. You are also blessed when they tell all kinds of evil lies about you because of me. Be joyful and glad. Your reward in heaven is great. In the same way, people hurt the prophets who lived long ago."

Jesus also taught the people how to pray by saying:

"When you pray, do not be like those who only pretend to be holy. They love to stand and pray in the synagogues and on the street corners. They want to be seen by other people. What I'm about to tell you is true. They have received their complete reward. When you pray, go into your room. Close the door and pray to your Father, who can't be seen. Your Father will reward you, because he sees what you do secretly. When you pray, do not keep talking on and on. That is what ungodly people do. They think they will be heard because they talk a lot. Do not be like them. Your Father knows what you need even before you ask him.

"This is how you should pray.

" 'Our Father in heaven,
may your name be honored.
May your kingdom come.
May what you want to happen be done
on earth as it is done in heaven.
Give us today our daily bread.
And forgive us our sins,
just as we also have forgiven those who
sin against us.
Keep us from sinning when we are
tempted.
Save us from the evil one.'

Forgive other people when they sin against you. If you do, your Father who is in heaven will also forgive you. But if you do not forgive the sins of other people, your Father will not forgive your sins."

Jesus told the people not to worry about anything, because God has a plan for everyone and promises to watch over us. Jesus said:

"I tell you, do not worry. Don't worry about your life and what you will eat or drink. And don't worry about your body and what you will wear. Isn't there more to life than eating? Aren't there more important things for the body than clothes? Look at the birds of the air. They don't plant or gather crops. They don't put away crops in storerooms. But your Father who is in heaven feeds them. Aren't you worth much more than they are? Can you add even one hour to your life by worrying?

"And why do you worry about clothes? See how the wild flowers grow. They don't work or make clothing. But here is what I tell you. Not even Solomon in all his royal robes was dressed like one of these flowers. If that is how God dresses the wild grass, won't he dress you even better? Your faith is so small! After all, the grass is here only today. Tomorrow it is thrown into the fire. So don't worry. Don't say, 'What will we eat?' Or, 'What will we drink?' Or, 'What will we wear?' People who are ungodly run after all those things. Your Father who is in heaven knows that you need them. But put God's kingdom first. Do what he wants you to do. Then all those things will also be given to you. So don't worry about tomorrow. Tomorrow will worry about itself. Each day has enough trouble of its own."

After Jesus taught the people these things, he and his disciples went out on a boat. The disciples were about to get a firsthand lesson about God's power.

When evening came, Jesus said to his disciples, "Let's go over to the other side of the lake." They left the crowd behind. And they took him along in a boat, just as he was. There were also other boats with him. A wild storm came up. Waves crashed over the boat. It was about to sink. Jesus was in the back, sleeping on a cushion. The disciples woke him up. They said, "Teacher! Don't you care if we drown?"

He got up and ordered the wind to stop. He said to the waves, "Quiet! Be still!" Then the wind died down. And it was completely calm.

He said to his disciples, "Why are you so afraid? Don't you have any faith at all yet?"

They were terrified. They asked each other, "Who is this? Even the wind and the waves obey him!"

Jesus could do more than stop the wind and the waves. Because he was God's son, Jesus could do miraculous things: he could heal people from deadly diseases and bring people back to life. Jesus also told his disciples to teach others about God and do miracles.

Jesus' miracles helped people believe his teachings were true. Jesus sent the twelve disciples out in groups of two. They preached, told people to confess their sins, and healed many people. Later ...

The apostles gathered around Jesus. They told him all they had done and taught. But many people were coming and going. So they did not even have a chance to eat. Then Jesus said to his apostles, "Come with me by yourselves to a quiet place. You need to get some rest."

So they went away by themselves in a boat to a quiet place. But many people who saw them leaving recognized them. They ran from all the towns and got there ahead of them. When Jesus came ashore, he saw a large crowd. He felt deep concern for them. They were like sheep without a shepherd. So he began teaching them many things.

By that time it was late in the day. His disciples came to him. "There is nothing here," they said. "It's already very late. Send the people away. Then they can go to the nearby country-side and villages to buy something to eat."

But Jesus answered, "You give them something to eat."

They said to him, "That would take more than half a year's pay! Should we go and spend that much on bread? Are we supposed to feed them?"

"How many loaves do you have?" Jesus asked. "Go and see."

When they found out, they said, "Five loaves and two fish."

Jesus took the five loaves and the two fish. He looked up to heaven and gave thanks. He broke the loaves into pieces. Then he gave them to his disciples to pass around to the people. He also divided the two fish among them all. All of them ate and were satisfied. The disciples picked up 12 baskets of broken pieces of bread and fish. The number of men who had eaten was 5,000.

Right away Jesus made the disciples get into the boat. He had them go on ahead of him to the other side of the Sea of Galilee. Then he sent the crowd away. After he had sent them away, he went up on a mountainside by himself to pray. Later that night, he was there alone. The boat was already a long way from land. It was being pounded by the waves because the wind was blowing against it.

Shortly before dawn, Jesus went out to the disciples. He walked on the lake. They saw him walking on the lake and were terrified. "It's a ghost!" they said. And they cried out in fear.

Right away Jesus called out to them, "Be brave! It is I. Don't be afraid."

"Lord, is it you?" Peter asked. "If it is, tell me to come to you on the water."

"Come," Jesus said.

So Peter got out of the boat. He walked on the water toward Jesus. But when Peter saw the wind, he was afraid. He began to sink. He cried out, "Lord! Save me!"

Right away Jesus reached out his hand and caught him. "Your faith is so small!" he said. "Why did you doubt me?"

When they climbed into the boat, the wind died down. Then those in the boat worshiped Jesus. They said, "You really are the Son of God!"

Some of the people who had eaten the bread and fish Jesus had multiplied found Jesus again. Jesus knew they were looking for him just because he did a miracle, not because they wanted to follow his teachings. Jesus told the people he was better than the miracle bread they had eaten. The miracle bread had filled their stomachs, but he was the bread of life, who would fill them spiritually and give them eternal life.

The people were confused by what Jesus said, because if Jesus was the bread of life, he was saying he came from heaven. They weren't sure they believed in Jesus anymore.

From this time on, many of his disciples turned back. They no longer followed him.

"You don't want to leave also, do you?" Jesus asked the 12 disciples.

Simon Peter answered him, "Lord, who can we go to? You have the words of eternal life. We have come to believe and to know that you are the Holy One of God."

Then Jesus replied, "Didn't I choose you, the 12 disciples? But one of you is a devil!" He meant Judas, the son of Simon Iscariot. Judas was one of the 12 disciples. But later he was going to hand Jesus over to his enemies.

Jesus was a good teacher, but that wasn't the only reason God put him on earth. For two years Jesus taught the people what God wanted them to do. Now the world was ready for the next part of God's plan—Jesus was going to show the people he was the Messiah they had been waiting for.

Discussion Questions

1. Have you ever helped a friend or sibling when they were hurting? Have you ever listened to them talk about their troubles? How does being the helper and listener make you feel?

2. What does it mean to you to have a "pure heart"?

3. Peter was afraid to get out of the boat and go to Jesus on the water. Have you ever tried something new even though you were afraid? What did you do? How did you get through it?

4

Jesus, the Son of God

Jesus had an important question for his apostles.

Jesus and his disciples went on to the villages around Caesarea Philippi. On the way he asked them, "Who do people say I am?"

They replied, "Some say John the Baptist. Others say Elijah. Still others say one of the prophets."

"But what about you?" he asked. "Who do you say I am?"

Peter answered, "You are the Messiah."

Jesus warned them not to tell anyone about him.

Jesus wanted to keep his real identity secret until the right time came. So Jesus kept teaching.

Jesus called the crowd to him along with his disciples. He said, "Whoever wants to be my disciple must say no to themselves. They must pick up their cross and follow me. Whoever wants to save their life will lose it. But whoever loses their life for me and for the good news will save it. What good is it if someone gains the whole world but loses their soul? Or what can anyone trade for their soul? Suppose anyone is ashamed of me and my words among these adulterous and sinful people. Then the Son of Man will be ashamed of them when he comes in his Father's glory with the holy angels."

During this time, Jesus spent a lot of time traveling with his disciples and teaching them who he was and what would happen to him.

Jesus did not want anyone to know where they were. That was because he was teaching his disciples. He said to them, "The Son of Man is going to be handed over to men. They will kill him. After three days he will rise from the dead." But they didn't understand what he meant. And they were afraid to ask him about it.

The disciples were having a hard time understanding Jesus' teachings because they still thought the Messiah would be a brave warrior or a fierce king who would save them from the Romans. They didn't understand that the Messiah would save them from their sins instead. And they didn't understand why Jesus had to die.

The Pharisees also had a hard time with Jesus' teachings—but they wanted to kill him. The Pharisees didn't like Jesus' teachings because they were different from what they thought. Jesus also wouldn't obey their rules, and he told people the Pharisees weren't always doing what God wanted. When it was time for the Feast of Tabernacles (a celebration of God's goodness), Jesus had to sneak into the city so the Pharisees wouldn't catch him.

At the feast the Jewish leaders were watching for Jesus. They were asking, "Where is he?"

Many people in the crowd were whispering about him. Some said, "He is a good man."

Others replied, "No. He fools the people." But no one would say anything about him openly. They were afraid of the leaders.

Jesus did nothing until halfway through the feast. Then he went up to the temple courtyard and began to teach. The Jews there were amazed. They asked, "How did this man learn so much without being taught?"

Then some of the people of Jerusalem began asking questions. They said, "Isn't this the man some people are trying to kill? Here he is! He is speaking openly. They aren't saying a word to him. Have the authorities really decided that he is the Messiah? But we know where this man is from. When the Messiah comes, no one will know where he is from."

Jesus was still teaching in the temple courtyard. He cried out, "Yes, you know me. And you know where I am from. I am not here on my own authority. The one who sent me is true.

You do not know him. But I know him. I am from him, and he sent me."

When he said this, they tried to arrest him. But no one laid a hand on him. The time for him to show who he really was had not yet come. Still, many people in the crowd believed in him. They said, "How will it be when the Messiah comes? Will he do more signs than this man?"

Jesus spoke to the people again. He said, "I am the light of the world. Anyone who follows me will never walk in darkness. They will have that light. They will have life."

The Pharisees argued with him. "Here you are," they said, "appearing as your own witness. But your witness does not count."

Jesus answered, "Even if I am a witness about myself, what I say does count. I know where I came from. And I know where I am going. But you have no idea where I come from or where I am going."

"If you obey my teaching," he said, "you are really my disciples. Then you will know the truth. And the truth will set you free."

A few months later, Jesus heard that his friend Lazarus had died. Jesus was very upset by the news, and he went to Lazarus's house.

When Jesus arrived, he found out that Lazarus had already been in the tomb for four days. Bethany was less than two miles from Jerusalem. Many Jews had come to Martha and Mary. They had come to comfort them because their brother was dead.

Once more Jesus felt very sad. He came to the tomb. It was a cave with a stone in front of the entrance. "Take away the stone," he said.

"But, Lord," said Martha, the sister of the dead man, "by this time there is a bad smell. Lazarus has been in the tomb for four days."

Then Jesus said, "Didn't I tell you that if you believe, you will see God's glory?"

So they took away the stone. Then Jesus looked up. He said, "Father, I thank you for hearing me. I know that you always hear me. But I said this for the benefit of the people standing here. I said it so they will believe that you sent me."

Then Jesus called in a loud voice. He said, "Lazarus, come out!" The dead man came out. His hands and feet were wrapped with strips of linen. A cloth was around his face.

Jesus said to them, "Take off the clothes he was buried in and let him go."

Many of the Jews who had come to visit Mary saw what Jesus did. So they believed in him. But some of them went to the Pharisees. They told the Pharisees what Jesus had done. Then the chief priests and the Pharisees called a meeting of the Sanhedrin.

"What can we do?" they asked. "This man is performing many signs. If we let him keep on doing this, everyone will believe in him. Then the Romans will come. They will take away our temple and our nation."

The leaders came up with a plan to get rid of Jesus for good. The Passover Feast was coming soon, and if Jesus came any-where near Jerusalem to celebrate, they would arrest him. Jesus knew the leaders wanted to kill him, but he started walking toward Jerusalem anyway.

People were bringing little children to Jesus. They wanted him to place his hands on them to bless them. But the disciples told them to stop. When Jesus saw this, he was angry. He said to his disciples, "Let the little children come to me. Don't keep them away. God's kingdom belongs to people like them. What I'm about to tell you is true. Anyone who will not receive God's kingdom like a little child will never enter it." Then he took the children in his arms. He placed his hands on them to bless them.

It was almost time for the Jewish Passover Feast. Many people went up from the country to Jerusalem. They went there for the special washing that would make them pure before the Passover Feast. They kept looking for Jesus as they stood in the temple courtyard. They asked one another, "What do you think? Isn't he coming to the feast at all?" But the chief priests and the Pharisees had given orders. They had commanded anyone who found out where Jesus was staying to report it. Then they could arrest him.

The time was finally right for everyone to know exactly who the Messiah was. Jesus was going to reveal that he was the Messiah to the people by walking into Jerusalem in a big parade. But first, Jesus had to send two of the disciples into Jerusalem to get something that would show the people he came in peace.

He said to them, "Go to the village ahead of you. Just as you enter it, you will find a donkey's colt tied there. No one has ever ridden it. Untie it and bring it here. Someone may ask you, 'Why are you doing this?' If so, say, 'The Lord needs it. But he will send it back here soon.'"

So they left. They found a colt out in the street. It was tied at a doorway. They untied it. Some people standing there asked, "What are you doing? Why are you untying that colt?" They answered as Jesus had told them to. So the people let them go. They brought the colt to Jesus. They threw their coats over it. Then he sat on it. Many people spread their coats on the road. Others spread branches they had cut in the fields. Those in front and those in back shouted,

"Hosanna!"

"Blessed is the one who comes in the
name of the Lord!"   *(Psalm 118:25,26)*

"Blessed is the coming kingdom of our
father David!"

"Hosanna in the highest heaven!"

When Jesus entered Jerusalem, the whole city was stirred up. The people asked, "Who is this?"

The crowds answered, "This is Jesus. He is the prophet from Nazareth in Galilee."

During Passover week, Jesus taught the people and told them he would have to die soon. Since he was human as well as God, Jesus was concerned with what he would have to face. Jesus said:

"My soul is troubled. What should I say? 'Father, keep me from having to go through with this'? No. This is the very reason I have come to this point in my life. Father, bring glory to your name!"

Then a voice came from heaven. It said, "I have brought glory to my name. I will bring glory to it again." The crowd there heard the voice. Some said it was thunder. Others said an angel had spoken to Jesus.

Jesus said, "This voice was for your benefit, not mine. Now it is time for the world to be judged. Now the prince of this world will be thrown out. And I am going to be lifted up from the earth. When I am, I will bring all people to

53

myself." He said this to show them how he was going to die.

Jesus had performed so many signs in front of them. But they still would not believe in him.

At the same time that Jesus did those signs, many of the Jewish leaders believed in him. But because of the Pharisees, they would not openly admit they believed. They were afraid they would be thrown out of the synagogue. They loved praise from people more than praise from God.

Then Jesus cried out, "Whoever believes in me does not believe in me only. They also believe in the one who sent me. The one who looks at me sees the one who sent me. I have come into the world to be its light. So no one who believes in me will stay in darkness.

"I don't judge a person who hears my words but does not obey them. I didn't come to judge the world. I came to save the world. But there is a judge for anyone who does not accept me and my words. These words I have spoken will judge them on the last day. I did not speak on my own. The Father who sent me commanded me to say all that I have said. I know that his command leads to eternal life. So everything I say is just what the Father has told me to say."

The Passover and the Feast of Unleavened Bread were only two days away. The chief priests and the teachers of the law were plotting to arrest Jesus secretly. They wanted to kill him. "But not during the feast," they said. "The people may stir up trouble."

The leaders were eager to kill Jesus, but they needed to figure out a good way to arrest him. One of Jesus' disciples, named Judas Iscariot, solved the leaders' problem. Judas decided he didn't want to follow Jesus anymore. So he went to talk to the leaders.

Then Satan entered Judas, who was called Iscariot. Judas was one of the 12 disciples. He went to the chief priests and the officers of the temple guard. He talked with them about how he could hand Jesus over to them. They were delighted and agreed to give him money. Judas accepted their offer. He watched for the right time to hand Jesus over to them. He wanted to do it when no crowd was around.

Discussion Questions

1. Some people say, "Hosanna!" when they praise Jesus. What do you say or sing when you praise Jesus?

2. Why do you think people didn't want to believe Jesus was the Savior?

3. Why do you think Jesus went back to Jerusalem, even though he knew some people wanted to kill him? Can you imagine believing in something that much?

5

The Hour of Darkness

It was the first day of the Feast of Unleavened Bread. That was the time to sacrifice the Passover lamb. Jesus' disciples asked him, "Where do you want us to go and prepare for you to eat the Passover meal?"

So he sent out two of his disciples. He told them, "Go into the city. A man carrying a jar of water will meet you. Follow him. He will enter a house. Say to its owner, 'The Teacher asks,

"Where is my guest room? Where can I eat the Passover meal with my disciples?" ' He will show you a large upstairs room. It will have furniture and will be ready. Prepare for us to eat there."

The disciples left and went into the city. They found things just as Jesus had told them. So they prepared the Passover meal.

When evening came, Jesus arrived with the 12 disciples.

While the disciples were eating their Passover meal, Jesus was thinking about what was going to happen to him. Then Jesus said something that really surprised the disciples.

Jesus' spirit was troubled. He said, "What I'm about to tell you is true. One of you is going to hand me over to my enemies."

His disciples stared at one another. They had no idea which one of them he meant.

"Lord, who is it?"

Jesus answered, "It is the one I will give this piece of bread to. I will give it to him after I have dipped it in the dish." He dipped the piece of bread. Then he gave it to Judas, son of Simon Iscariot. As soon as Judas took the bread, Satan entered into him.

So Jesus told him, "Do quickly what you are going to do." But no one at the meal understood why Jesus said this to him. Judas was in charge of the money. So some of the disciples thought Jesus was telling him to buy what was needed for the feast. Others thought Jesus was talking about giving something to poor people. As soon as Judas had taken the bread, he went out. And it was night.

After Judas left, Jesus told the disciples what was going to happen. He explained that his body would be broken like the bread, and his blood would be poured out like the wine.

While they were eating, Jesus took bread. He gave thanks and broke it. He handed it to his disciples and said, "Take this and eat it. This is my body."

Then he took a cup. He gave thanks and handed it to them. He said, "All of you drink from it. This is my blood of the covenant. It is poured out to forgive the sins of many people."

"Do not let your hearts be troubled. You believe in God. Believe in me also. There are many rooms in my Father's house. If this were not true, would I have told you that I am going there? Would I have told you that I would prepare a place for you there? If I go and do that, I will come back. And I will take you to be with me. Then you will also be where I am. You know the way to the place where I am going."

Thomas said to him, "Lord, we don't know

where you are going. So how can we know the way?"

Jesus answered, "I am the way and the truth and the life. No one comes to the Father except through me. If you really know me, you will know my Father also. From now on, you do know him. And you have seen him."

Philip said, "Lord, show us the Father. That will be enough for us."

Jesus answered, "Don't you know me, Philip? I have been among you such a long time! Anyone who has seen me has seen the Father. So how can you say, 'Show us the Father'? Don't you believe that I am in the Father? Don't you believe that the Father is in me? The words I say to you I do not speak on my own authority. The Father lives in me. He is the one who is doing his work. Believe me when I say I am in the Father. Also believe that the Father is in me. Or at least believe what the works I have been doing say about me. What I'm about to tell you is true. Anyone who believes in me will do the works I have been doing. In fact, they will do even greater things. That's because I am going to the Father. And I will do anything you ask in my name. Then the Father will receive glory from the Son. You may ask me for anything in my name. I will do it.

"If you love me, obey my commands."

Jesus tried to help his disciples under-stand what was going to happen to him, but he knew the disciples would still get scared. He said that some of the disciples might run away when the soldiers came, and that they would even tell people they didn't know Jesus so they wouldn't get hurt. But a disciple named Peter was feel-ing brave.

Peter replied, "All the others may turn away because of you. But I never will."

"What I'm about to tell you is true," Jesus answered. "It will happen tonight. Before the rooster crows, you will say three times that you don't know me."

But Peter said, "I may have to die with you. But I will never say I don't know you." And all the other disciples said the same thing.

Then Jesus went with his disciples to a place called Gethsemane. He said to them, "Sit here while I go over there and pray." He took Peter and the two sons of Zebedee along with him. He began to be sad and troubled. Then he said to them, "My soul is very sad. I feel close to death. Stay here. Keep watch with me."

He went a little farther. Then he fell with his face to the ground. He prayed, "My Father, if it is possible, take this cup of suffering away from me. But let what you want be done, not what I want."

Then he returned to his disciples and found them sleeping. "Couldn't you men keep watch with me for one hour?" he asked Peter. "Watch and pray. Then you won't fall into sin when you are tempted. The spirit is willing, but the body is weak."

Jesus went away a second time. He prayed, "My Father, is it possible for this cup to be taken away? But if I must drink it, may what you want be done."

An angel from heaven appeared to Jesus and gave him strength. Because he was very sad and troubled, he prayed even harder. His sweat was like drops of blood falling to the ground.

Then he came back. Again he found them sleeping. They couldn't keep their eyes open.

So he left them and went away once more. For the third time he prayed the same thing.

Then he returned to the disciples. He said to them, "Are you still sleeping and resting? Look! The hour has come. The Son of Man is about to be handed over to sinners. Get up! Let us go! Here comes the one who is handing me over to them!"

While Jesus was still speaking, Judas arrived. He was one of the 12 disciples. A large crowd was with him. They were carrying swords and clubs. The chief priests and the elders of the people had sent them.

Jesus knew everything that was going to happen to him. So he went out and asked them, "Who do you want?"

"Jesus of Nazareth," they replied.

"I am he," Jesus said. Judas, who was going to hand Jesus over, was standing there with them. When Jesus said, "I am he," they moved back. Then they fell to the ground.

He asked them again, "Who do you want?"

"Jesus of Nazareth," they said.

Jesus answered, "I told you I am he. If you are looking for me, then let these men go." This happened so that the words Jesus had spoken would come true. He had said, "I have not lost anyone God has given me." *(John 6:39)*

Simon Peter had a sword and pulled it out. He struck the high priest's slave and cut off his right ear.

But Jesus answered, "Stop this!" And he touched the man's ear and healed him.

Jesus knew that these bad things had to happen to make sure everything the prophets had said about the Messiah came true. So he didn't resist being arrested. After the soldiers arrested Jesus, the disciples ran away, just like Jesus had predicted. The soldiers took Jesus to the leaders, who put him on trial. One disciple named Peter secretly followed the soldiers and waited outside so he would know how the trial was going.

Some people there started a fire in the middle of the courtyard. Then they sat down together. Peter sat down with them. A female servant saw him sitting there in the firelight. She looked closely at him. Then she said, "This man was with Jesus."

But Peter said he had not been with him. "Woman, I don't know him," he said.

A little later someone else saw Peter. "You also are one of them," he said.

"No," Peter replied. "I'm not!"

About an hour later, another person spoke up. "This fellow must have been with Jesus," he said. "He is from Galilee."

Peter replied, "Man, I don't know what you're talking about!" Just as he was speaking, the rooster crowed. The Lord turned and looked right at Peter. Then Peter remembered what the Lord had spoken to him. "The rooster will crow today," Jesus had said. "Before it does, you will say three times that you don't know me." Peter went outside. He broke down and cried.

During the trial, the leaders found a reason to put Jesus to death. Jesus told the leaders he was God's Son, but the leaders thought he was lying. According to the leaders' rules, people who lied about being God had to die. Since the leaders couldn't kill Jesus themselves, they took him to a Roman governor named Pilate.

Pilate knew Jesus hadn't done anything wrong, but he still said Jesus had to die.

Then Pilate took Jesus and had him whipped. The soldiers twisted thorns together to make a crown. They put it on Jesus' head. Then they put a purple robe on him. They went up to him again and again. They kept saying, "We honor you, king of the Jews!" And they slapped him in the face.

Once more Pilate came out. He said to the Jews gathered there, "Look, I am bringing Jesus out to you. I want to let you know that I find no basis for a charge against him." Jesus came out wearing the crown of thorns and the purple robe. Then Pilate said to them, "Here is the man!"

As soon as the chief priests and their officials saw him, they shouted, "Crucify him! Crucify him!"

But Pilate answered, "You take him and crucify him. I myself find no basis for a charge against him."

The Jewish leaders replied, "We have a law. That law says he must die. He claimed to be the Son of God."

Finally, Pilate handed Jesus over to them to be nailed to a cross.

On their way out of the city, they met a man from Cyrene. His name was Simon. They forced him to carry the cross.

Two other men were also led out with Jesus to be killed. Both of them had broken the law. The soldiers brought them to the place called the Skull. There they nailed Jesus to the cross. He hung between the two criminals. One was on his right and one was on his left. Jesus said, "Father, forgive them. They don't know what they are doing." The soldiers divided up his clothes by casting lots.

The people stood there watching. The rulers even made fun of Jesus. They said, "He saved others. Let him save himself if he is God's Messiah, the Chosen One."

The soldiers also came up and poked fun at him. They offered him wine vinegar. They said, "If you are the king of the Jews, save yourself."

A written sign had been placed above him. It read,

THIS IS THE KING OF THE JEWS.

One of the criminals hanging there made fun of Jesus. He said, "Aren't you the Messiah? Save yourself! Save us!"

But the other criminal scolded him. "Don't you have any respect for God?" he said. "Remember, you are under the same sentence of death. We are being punished fairly. We are getting just what our actions call for. But this man hasn't done anything wrong."

Then he said, "Jesus, remember me when you come into your kingdom."

Jesus answered him, "What I'm about to tell you is true. Today you will be with me in paradise."

For long, painful hours, Jesus hung on the cross. Not only did his hands and feet hurt where nails had been pounded into him, but breathing was very hard. Jesus had to pull himself up with his tired, painful arms each time he had to breathe, and as time passed he had less and less energy and more and more pain to deal with.

It was now about noon. Then darkness covered the whole land until three o'clock. The sun had stopped shining.

About three o'clock, Jesus cried out in a loud voice. He said, "*Eli, Eli, lema sabachthani?*" This means "My God, my God, why have you deserted me?" *(Psalm 22:1)*

Some of those standing there heard Jesus cry out. They said, "He's calling for Elijah."

Right away one of them ran and got a sponge. He filled it with wine vinegar and put it on a stick. He offered it to Jesus to drink. The rest said, "Leave him alone. Let's see if Elijah comes to save him."

After Jesus drank he said, "It is finished." Then he bowed his head and died.

At that moment the temple curtain was torn in two from top to bottom. The earth shook. The rocks split. Tombs broke open. The bodies of many holy people who had died were raised to life. They came out of the tombs. After Jesus was raised from the dead, they went into the holy city. There they appeared to many people.

The Roman commander and those guarding Jesus saw the earthquake and all that had happened. They were terrified. They exclaimed, "He was surely the Son of God!"

The people had gathered to watch this sight. When they saw what happened, they felt very sad. Then they went away. But all those who knew Jesus stood not very far away, watching these things. They included the women who had followed him from Galilee.

Discussion Questions

1. How is communion celebrated at your church (or at the churches you have visited)?

2. Peter denied knowing Jesus three times. Do you think you would have denied knowing Jesus? Do you tell others that you believe in Jesus?

3. Why did Jesus die for our sins?

6

The Resurrection

Jesus was dead, and his followers were incredibly sad. They forgot Jesus said he wouldn't stay dead forever. Once Jesus' body was taken down off the cross, two of Jesus' friends buried it in a cave tomb. Then they rolled a large, heavy stone in front of the opening to close it.

But the Jewish leaders remembered that Jesus promised to come back to life in three days. They put soldiers in front of the tomb to make sure no one tried to steal Jesus' body to pretend he was alive. No

one really thought Jesus would come back
to life. But on the morning of the third day,
something surprising happened.

There was a powerful earthquake. An angel of the Lord came down from heaven. The angel went to the tomb. He rolled back the stone and sat on it. His body shone like lightning. His clothes were as white as snow. The guards were so afraid of him that they shook and became like dead men.

The angel said to the women, "Don't be afraid. I know that you are looking for Jesus, who was crucified. He is not here! He has risen, just as he said he would! Come and see the place where he was lying. Go quickly! Tell his disciples, 'He has risen from the dead. He is going ahead of you into Galilee. There you will see him.' Now I have told you."

So the women hurried away from the tomb. They were afraid, but they were filled with joy. They ran to tell the disciples.

So Peter and the other disciple started out for the tomb. Both of them were running. The other disciple ran faster than Peter. He reached the tomb first. He bent over and looked in at the strips of linen lying there. But he did not go in. Then Simon Peter came along behind him. He went straight into the tomb. He saw the strips of linen lying there. He also saw the funeral cloth that had been wrapped around Jesus' head. The cloth was still lying in its place. It was separate from the linen. The disciple who had reached the tomb first also went inside. He saw and believed. They still did not understand from Scripture that Jesus had to rise from the dead. Then the disciples went back to where they were staying.

The disciples were still talking about this when Jesus himself suddenly stood among them. He said, "May you have peace!"

They were surprised and terrified. They thought they were seeing a ghost. Jesus said to them, "Why are you troubled? Why do you have doubts in your minds? Look at my hands and my feet. It's really me! Touch me and see. A ghost does not have a body or bones. But you can see that I do."

After he said that, he showed them his hands and feet. But they still did not believe it.

They were amazed and filled with joy. So Jesus asked them, "Do you have anything here to eat?" They gave him a piece of cooked fish. He took it and ate it in front of them.

Jesus said to them, "This is what I told you while I was still with you. Everything written about me in the Law of Moses, the Prophets and the Psalms must come true."

Then he opened their minds so they could understand the Scriptures. He told them, "This is what is written. The Messiah will suffer. He will rise from the dead on the third day. His followers will preach in his name. They will tell others to turn away from their sins and be forgiven. People from every nation will hear it, beginning at Jerusalem. You have seen these things with your own eyes. I am going to send you what my Father has promised. But for now, stay in the city. Stay there until you have received power from heaven."

After this, Jesus appeared to his disciples again. It was by the Sea of Galilee. Here is what happened. Simon Peter and Thomas, who was also called Didymus, were there together. Nathanael from Cana in Galilee and the sons of Zebedee were with them. So were two other disciples. "I'm going out to fish," Simon Peter told them. They said, "We'll go with you." So they went out and got into the boat. That night they didn't catch anything.

Early in the morning, Jesus stood on the shore. But the disciples did not realize that it was Jesus.

He called out to them, "Friends, don't you have any fish?"

"No," they answered.

He said, "Throw your net on the right side of

the boat. There you will find some fish." When they did, they could not pull the net into the boat. There were too many fish in it.

It took a while for the disciples to really understand Jesus was back, and what his resurrection meant. Jesus reminded them of his teachings so things would make sense to them. The disciples needed to know why Jesus died and came back to life because they would need to tell everyone else what they had seen and heard.

Then the 11 disciples went to Galilee. They went to the mountain where Jesus had told them to go. When they saw him, they worshiped him. But some still had their doubts. Then Jesus came to them. He said, "All authority in heaven and on earth has been given to me. So you must go and make disciples of all nations. Baptize them in the name of the Father and of the Son and of the Holy Spirit. Teach them to obey everything I have commanded you. And you can be sure that I am always with you, to the very end."

Discussion Questions

1. Why do you think Jesus was resurrected from the dead?

2. How do you think Jesus knew there were all those fish on the other side of the boat? Do you believe in miracles? Have you ever experienced a miracle or heard about someone else experiencing a miracle?

3. How can you tell or show others about what Jesus taught the disciples?

7

New Beginnings

Before Jesus left, he gave orders to the apostles he had chosen. He did this through the Holy Spirit. After his suffering and death, he appeared to them. In many ways he proved that he was alive. He appeared to them over a period of 40 days. During that time he spoke about God's kingdom. One day Jesus was eating with them. He gave them a command. "Do not leave Jerusalem," he said. "Wait for the gift my Father promised. You have heard me talk about it. John baptized with water. But in a few days you will be baptized with the Holy Spirit."

Then the apostles gathered around Jesus and asked him a question. "Lord," they said, "are you going to give the kingdom back to Israel now?"

He said to them, "You should not be concerned about times or dates. The Father has set them by his own authority. But you will receive power when the Holy Spirit comes on you. Then you will tell people about me in Jerusalem, and in all Judea and Samaria. And you will even tell other people about me from one end of the earth to the other."

After Jesus said this, he was taken up to heaven. The apostles watched until a cloud hid him from their sight.

While he was going up, they kept on looking at the sky. Suddenly two men dressed in white clothing stood beside them. "Men of Galilee," they said, "why do you stand here looking at the sky? Jesus has been taken away from you into heaven. But he will come back in the same way you saw him go."

When the day of Pentecost came, all the believers gathered in one place. Suddenly a sound came from heaven. It was like a strong wind blowing. It filled the whole house where they were sitting. They saw something that looked like fire in the shape of tongues. The flames separated and came to rest on each of them. All of them were filled with the Holy Spirit. They began to speak in languages they had not known before. The Spirit gave them the ability to do this.

Godly Jews from every country in the world were staying in Jerusalem. A crowd came together when they heard the sound. They were bewildered because each of them heard their own language being spoken.

The Holy Spirit came to help the disciples tell people about Jesus and help others believe in Jesus too. But some of the people thought the disciples were just acting crazy. So Peter started telling the crowd all the facts about Jesus.

"Long ago God planned that Jesus would be handed over to you. With the help of evil people, you put Jesus to death. You nailed him to the cross. But God raised him from the dead. He set him free from the suffering of death. It wasn't possible for death to keep its hold on Jesus."

"God has raised this same Jesus back to life. We are all witnesses of this. Jesus has been given a place of honor at the right hand of God. He has received the Holy Spirit from the Father. This is what God had promised. It is Jesus who has poured out what you now see and hear."

Many people became believers of Jesus because of what the apostles taught them.

The believers studied what the apostles taught. They shared their lives together. They ate and prayed together. Everyone was amazed at what God was doing. They were amazed when the apostles performed many wonders and signs. All the believers were together. They shared everything they had. They sold property and other things they owned. They gave to anyone who needed something. Every day they met together in the temple courtyard. They ate meals together in their homes. Their hearts were glad and sincere. They praised God. They were respected by all the people. Every day the Lord added to their group those who were being saved.

The leaders who hated Jesus didn't like Jesus' followers either. A man named Saul

and other Jewish leaders tried to stop the
church of believers from adding new people
by scaring or even killing them. Many Chris-
tians went to other cities so they would be
safe, and there they told others about Jesus.

The believers who had been scattered preached the word everywhere they went. Philip went down to a city in Samaria. There he preached about the Messiah. The crowds listened to Philip and saw the signs he did. All of them paid close attention to what he said. Evil spirits screamed and came out of many people. Many people who were disabled or who couldn't walk were healed. So there was great joy in that city.

Meanwhile, Saul continued to oppose the Lord's followers. He said they would be put to death. He went to the high priest. He asked the priest for letters to the synagogues in Damascus. He wanted to find men and women who belonged to the Way of Jesus. The letters would allow him to take them as prisoners to Jerusalem. On his journey, Saul approached Damascus. Suddenly a light from heaven flashed around him. He fell to the ground. He heard a voice speak to him, "Saul! Saul! Why are you opposing me?"

"Who are you, Lord?" Saul asked.

"I am Jesus," he replied. "I am the one you are opposing. Now get up and go into the city. There you will be told what you must do."

The men traveling with Saul stood there. They weren't able to speak. They had heard the sound. But they didn't see anyone. Saul got up from the ground. He opened his eyes, but he couldn't see. So they led him by the hand into Damascus. For three days he was blind. He didn't eat or drink anything.

In Damascus there was a believer named Ananias. The Lord called out to him in a vision. "Ananias!" he said.

"Yes, Lord," he answered.

The Lord told him, "Go to the house of Judas on Straight Street. Ask for a man from Tarsus named Saul. He is praying. In a vision Saul has seen a man come and place his hands on him. That man's name is Ananias. In the vision, Ananias placed his hands on Saul so he could see again."

"Lord," Ananias answered, "I've heard many reports about this man. They say he has done great harm to your holy people in Jerusalem. Now he has come here to arrest all those who worship you. The chief priests have given him authority to do this."

But the Lord said to Ananias, "Go! I have chosen this man to work for me. He will announce my name to the Gentiles and to their kings. He will also announce my name to the people of Israel. I will show him how much he must suffer for me."

Then Ananias went to the house and entered it. He placed his hands on Saul. "Brother Saul," he said, "you saw the Lord Jesus. He appeared to you on the road as you were coming here. He has sent me so that you will be able to see again. You will be filled with the Holy Spirit." Right away something like scales fell from Saul's eyes. And he could see again. He got up and was baptized. After eating some food, he got his strength back.

Saul's heart had completely changed. Saul started telling people about Jesus, and he changed his name to Paul to show he was a different person. After a while he went to Jerusalem to talk to the disciples (who were now called the apostles) about how he could help the church. The apostles realized Paul really did love Jesus, and that he was a very good preacher. At the direction of the Holy Spirit, they decided to send Paul to other countries to tell the non-Jewish people about Jesus—just like God said would happen.

About this time, King Herod arrested some people who belonged to the church. He planned to make them suffer greatly. He had James killed with a sword. James was John's brother. Herod saw that the death of James pleased some Jews. So he arrested Peter also. This happened during the Feast of Unleavened Bread. After Herod arrested Peter, he put him in prison. Peter was placed under guard. He was watched by four groups of four soldiers each. Herod planned to put Peter on public trial. It would take place after the Passover Feast.

So Peter was kept in prison. But the church prayed hard to God for him.

It was the night before Herod was going to bring him to trial. Peter was sleeping between two soldiers. Two chains held him there. Lookouts stood guard at the entrance. Suddenly an angel of the Lord appeared. A light shone in the prison cell. The angel struck Peter on his side. Peter woke up. "Quick!" the angel said. "Get up!" The chains fell off Peter's wrists.

Then the angel said to him, "Put on your clothes and sandals." Peter did so. "Put on your coat," the angel told him. "Follow me." Peter followed him out of the prison. But he had no idea that what the angel was doing was really happening. He thought he was seeing a vision. They passed the first and second guards. Then they came to the iron gate leading to the city. It opened for them by itself. They went through it. They walked the length of one street. Suddenly the angel left Peter.

Then Peter realized what had happened. He said, "Now I know for sure that the Lord has sent his angel. He set me free from Herod's power. He saved me from everything the Jewish people were hoping would happen."

When Peter understood what had happened, he went to Mary's house. Mary was the mother of John Mark. Many people had gathered in her home. They were praying there. Peter knocked at the outer entrance. A servant named Rhoda came to answer the door. She recognized Peter's voice. She was so excited that she ran back without opening the door. "Peter is at the door!" she exclaimed.

"You're out of your mind," they said to her. But she kept telling them it was true. So they said, "It must be his angel."

Peter kept on knocking. When they opened the door and saw him, they were amazed. Peter motioned with his hand for them to be quiet. He explained how the Lord had brought him out of prison. "Tell James and the other brothers and sisters about this," he said. Then he went to another place.

In the morning the soldiers were bewildered. They couldn't figure out what had happened to Peter.

No matter who hurt the new Christians, the Holy Spirit continued to work in the new believers, encouraging them to spread the Good News. Saul (Paul) and his co-workers boldly spoke about Jesus everywhere they went.

Discussion Questions

1. What do you think angels look like? Where did you get your ideas?

2. What does the Holy Spirit mean to you?

3. How can you show others that you are a Christian?

List of Bible Excerpts

Chapter 1: The Birth of the King

John 1:1–5, 9–14, 17–18
Luke 1:26–35, 38, 46–55
Matthew 1:19–24

Luke 2:1, 3–20
Matthew 2:1–3
Luke 2:41–52

Chapter 2: Jesus' Ministry Begins

Matthew 3:1–2, 4–6,
   13–17
Matthew 4:1–11
John 1:19–34
Mark 1:31–34, 40–45

Mark 2:1–12
Matthew 4:24–25
Mark 3:9–12, 13–15
Luke 8:1–3

Chapter 3: No Ordinary Man

Mark 4:30–34
Luke 15:1–7
Luke 10:25–37
Matthew 5:2–12
Matthew 6:5–15

Matthew 6:25–34
Mark 4:35–41
Mark 6:30–38, 41–44
Matthew 14:22–33
John 6:66–71

Chapter 4: Jesus, the Son of God

Mark 8:27–30, 34–38
Mark 9:30–32
John 7:11–15, 25–31
John 8:12–14, 31–32
John 11:17–19, 38–48
Mark 10:13–16
John 11:55–57

Mark 11:2–10
Matthew 21:10–11
John 12:27–33, 37,
   42–50
Mark 14:1–2
Luke 22:3–6

Chapter 5: The Hour of Darkness

Mark 14:12–17
John 13:21–22, 25–30
Matthew 26:26–28
John 14:1–15
Matthew 26:33–42
Luke 22:43–44
Matthew 26:43–47
John 18:4–10

Luke 22:51, 55–62
John 19:1–7, 16
Matthew 27:32
Luke 23:32–45
Matthew 27:46–49
John 19:30
Matthew 27:51–54
Luke 23:48–49

Chapter 6: The Resurrection

Matthew 28:2–8
John 20:3–10
Luke 24:36–49

John 21:1–6
Matthew 28:16–20

Chapter 7: New Beginnings

Acts 1:2–11
Acts 2:1–6, 23–24, 32–33, 42–47
Acts 8:4–8

Acts 9:1–19
Acts 12:1–18

Adventure.

Humor.

Drama.

The Story for Kids, NIrV
Discover the Bible from
Beginning to End

Now kids can discover God's great love
story in a new format! As you read, you
will uncover the "big picture." You'll
find out that God's story is not just a
collection of random adventures—it's
a complete story that tells about God's
great love for his people. Using the
New International Reader's Version
(NIrV) of the Bible, *The Story for Kids*

Softcover:
978-0-310-74436-8

reads like a novel. Events, characters, and teachings are
arranged in order to show God's unfolding story. This revised
edition has updated transitions and all-new artwork.

You'll love reading the greatest story ever told!

Visit your local retailer to purchase
or TheStory.com for more info.

THE STORY

POWERED BY ZONDERVAN

ENJOY GOD'S WORD AS A FAMILY!
The Story Helps All Ages Understand The Bible

The Story is a whole new way of experiencing the Bible. From Creation to Revelation, you'll read 31 chapters of scripture that reads like a novel. You and your family will grow in your understanding and enthusiasm for God's Word as you read *The Story* together and learn how your individual stories intersect with God's story.

Age 18 and up

Age 12-18

Age 2-5

Age 4-8

Age 9-12

Available Family Pack includes *The Story*, *The Story for Kids*, and *The Story For Children*. See your local Christian retailer.

NIV NEW INTERNATIONAL VERSION

THE STORY
POWERED BY ZONDERVAN

TURN EVERYDAY PEOPLE INTO DEVOTED BIBLE READERS

Limited Time Offer!
$149.99
A $300 Value

The Story Church-Wide Experience: Bible Engagement for Adults, Teens, and Children

Thousands of pastors trust Zondervan's *The Story* to help people experience Scripture like never before. Carefully selected verses from the Bible are organized chronologically and read like a novel. From Genesis to Revelation, congregants of all ages learn God's story and how their stories intersect with it.

Affordable, flexible and easy-to-use, churches are using *The Story* as a powerful church-wide experience and in individual ministries such as small groups, Sunday School and youth ministry.

THE STORY KIT INCLUDES:

- *The Story*—Book and Adult Curriculum
- *The Story, Teen Edition*—Book and Curriculum
- *The Story for Kids*—Book and Curriculum
- *The Story for Children*—Book and Curriculum
- *The Story for Little Ones*—Book and Curriculum
- *The Heart of the Story*—by Randy Frazee
- *The Story* Resource DVD-ROM
- Access to *The Story* Online Resource Library
- Implementation Guide

Church Campaign Kit
9780310941538
$149.99 ($300 Value)

NIV

THE STORY
POWERED BY ZONDERVAN